The Coronavirus Pandemic of 2020

Kathleen DuVall

ReferencePoint
Press®

San Diego, CA

About the Author

Kathleen DuVall is an editor and writer in Richmond, Virginia.

© 2022 ReferencePoint Press, Inc.
Printed in the United States

For more information, contact:
ReferencePoint Press, Inc.
PO Box 27779
San Diego, CA 92198
www.ReferencePointPress.com

LIBRARY OF CONGRESS CATALOGING-IN-PUBLICATION DATA

Names: DuVall, Kathleen, author.
Title: The coronavirus pandemic of 2020 / Kathleen DuVall.
Description: San Diego, CA : ReferencePoint Press, 2022. | Series: Historic pandemics and plagues | Includes bibliographical references and index.
Identifiers: LCCN 2021016084 (print) | LCCN 2021016085 (ebook) | ISBN 9781678201005 (library binding) | ISBN 9781678201012 (ebook)
Subjects: LCSH: COVID-19 (Disease) | COVID-19 (Disease)--Prevention. | COVID-19 (Disease)--Treatment. | COVID-19 (Disease)--History.
Classification: LCC RA644.C67 D883 2022 (print) | LCC RA644.C67 (ebook) | DDC 614.5/92414--dc23
LC record available at https://lccn.loc.gov/2021016084
LC ebook record available at https://lccn.loc.gov/2021016085

CONTENTS

Important Events During the
Coronavirus Pandemic   4

Introduction   6
The Coronavirus Emerged

Chapter One   10
The Coronavirus Circled the Globe

Chapter Two   22
A Year of Pandemic Suffering

Chapter Three   32
Pandemic Shock to the Global Economy

Chapter Four   43
Vaccines to the Rescue

Source Notes   55
For Further Research   58
Index   61
Picture Credits   64

Important Events During the Coronavirus Pandemic

January 2020
On January 10 scientists release the complete genetic blueprint of the new coronavirus.

On January 30 scientists confirm asymptomatic spread of the coronavirus and WHO declares a global health emergency.

April 2020
On April 10 coronavirus cases surge in Russia. By April 26 the pandemic has killed more than 200,000 and sickened more than 2.8 million worldwide.

December 2019
First COVID-19 hospital admission occurs on December 16 in Wuhan, China.

May 2020
By May 27 the United States has more than 100,000 COVID-19 deaths, surpassing all other nations.

2019   2020

February 2020
On February 11 WHO officially names the disease caused by the new coronavirus COVID-19.

Series of stock market crashes begins on February 20, marking the start of a worldwide economic recession.

Europe's first major outbreak occurs in Italy on February 23; three days later, Brazil reports Latin America's first known case of coronavirus.

March 2020
On March 24 officials announce postponement of the 2020 Tokyo Summer Olympics.

On March 26 the United States becomes the world leader in coronavirus infections when the nation's case count surpasses 100,000.

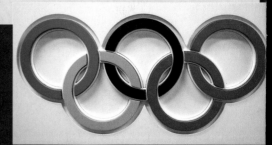

May 2021

As coronavirus infect
and deaths fall in
countries with aggres
vaccination campaigr
India experiences a
dangerous resurgeno
both. On May 5 the I
government announc
357,000 new infectio
and 3,449 deaths ov
previous twenty-four

July 2020

On July 8 scientists
confirm airborne
transmission of the
coronavirus that causes
COVID-19.

October 2020

On October 1
the US president
is hospitalized
for COVID-19.

August 2020

Scientists confirm
the existence
of a new, more
contagious strain
of coronavirus.

November 2020

On November 8 the
world passes 50 million
coronavirus cases.

2021

September 2020

On September 8
nine of the leading
drug companies de-
veloping COVID-19
vaccines pledge in
writing to put safety
before speed.

December 2020

The FDA issues Emergency Use
Authorization for the Pfizer-BioNTech
vaccine on December 11 and for the
Moderna vaccine on December 18.

By December 31 about 10 million vaccines
have been administered worldwide.

e 2020

June 4 large spikes
reported in the Middle
st, Latin America,
ca, and South Asia—all
vhich had been mostly
red until this time.

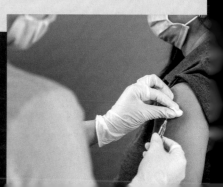

The Coronavirus Emerged

The trouble began in December 2019 in Wuhan, a large city in China's Hubei Province. In the beginning, the doctors in Wuhan only knew that there was a mysterious pneumonia, an infection of the lungs that affected the breathing of those who were ill. There were only a few cases at first, but when more and more sick people came to the hospitals with fever and difficulty breathing, doctors took notice and set out to find the reason, asking some basic questions: What caused this illness? How did the sick people acquire it? Did it spread from person to person? If so, how did it spread?

Finding the Cause of COVID-19

Finding the cause of an illness first involves ruling out possible causes. There are many known causes of lung problems, including cigarette smoking and air pollution. People who work in coal mines, for example, breathe in coal dust, which is harmful and can lead to lung disease. But the sick people in Wuhan did not work in such hazardous places or—as far as the doctors knew—have any exposure to hazards in their environment.

Pathogens—germs—also cause respiratory illness. This was a more likely explanation, and to test the idea, doctors gathered evidence. They examined samples of mucus from the sick people under a microscope and found the answer: the sick people were infected with a coronavirus, a type of virus named for its shape. The coronavirus is covered with protein spikes that make it look, under the microscope, somewhat like a crown (in Latin: corona).

Coronaviruses are not uncommon, and often they are not harmful. But this was a new (novel) coronavirus, and because of its newness, it could be dangerous. Without immunity to the new virus, people around the world were vulnerable.

When a new pathogen emerges, it presents a serious problem—the human immune system is not equipped to fight it, and there are no vaccines to provide protection. Because there were few natural or scientific defenses against the new coronavirus, it sickened and killed people as it spread around the world.

Zhang Yongzhen, a Chinese virologist in Shanghai, was familiar with coronaviruses from his work with severe acute respiratory syndrome (SARS), a deadly disease that had surfaced in China in 2003. As Zhang studied the new virus, he made some important observations: "One, it was like SARS. Two, it was a new coronavirus. Most important, the virus was transmitted through the respiratory tract. I also thought it was more infectious than the flu virus. Even then, I thought it must be able to spread from humans to humans."[1] Zhang was right.

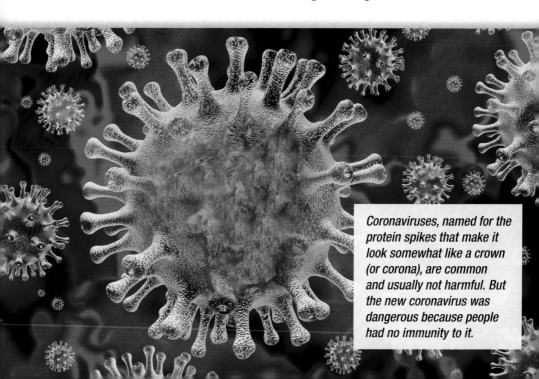

Coronaviruses, named for the protein spikes that make it look somewhat like a crown (or corona), are common and usually not harmful. But the new coronavirus was dangerous because people had no immunity to it.

How Did the New Coronavirus Spread?

Some of the people who fell ill had connections to a particular seafood market in Wuhan, where wild animals were sold for food. It is possible that the sick people in Wuhan had been infected through animals at the market. But was it passing from one person to another? Animal coronaviruses had only rarely infected humans and spread from there to other humans, but it had happened before—most recently in 2003 with the SARS coronavirus. Scientists suspected, and quickly confirmed as they examined the evidence, that the new coronavirus was passing directly from one person to another—human-to-human transmission.

Once the coronavirus was identified and human-to-human transmission confirmed, scientists developed a hypothesis. They theorized that COVID-19 probably spread as SARS had spread and as many respiratory diseases spread—through close contact with a sick person, such as by kissing, sharing food, or being nearby when a sick person coughs or sneezes. This hypothesis was refined as more evidence emerged. Through observation and experimentation, scientists identified smaller, airborne droplets that traveled farther and stayed in the air longer than previously thought. The coronavirus was spreading among people who were talking or even just breathing together in enclosed spaces. And another characteristic of the new coronavirus made it particularly dangerous: asymptomatic spread. Scientists would soon discover that the coronavirus was being spread by people who had no symptoms.

Zhang and other scientists in China understood that the only way to stop the coronavirus was to share information with other scientists around the world. In mid-January 2020 they shared the genome sequence of the coronavirus publicly so that scientists around the world could work on developing treatments and vaccines. The World Health Organization (WHO) gave the new variation of coronavirus an official name: SARS-CoV-2 (severe acute respiratory syndrome coronavirus 2). The disease caused by the coronavirus was also given an official name: COVID-19 (coronavirus disease 2019).

Science Versus COVID-19 in 2020

By late January 2020 at least thirteen countries were reporting cases of COVID-19, and eighty-one people were known to have died from it. Doctors and scientists worldwide knew they were in a race to save lives. They needed to prevent the spread of the coronavirus, find treatments for COVID-19, develop a vaccine, and distribute it to people all over the globe. All these things take time. By the end of 2020, scientists and doctors had resolved some of the questions about COVID-19. They understood better how the coronavirus spread and how it damaged the human body. Using the knowledge they had gained over the year, they had developed ways to prevent and treat COVID-19. There was no cure, but vaccines were in the works.

All the progress against the coronavirus in 2020 was made because of science. Science requires observation, looking closely at a problem from all sides, gathering information, and documenting the details. Scientists try to avoid making assumptions, which are sometimes wrong. They ask a question: what is causing this disease? They notice patterns and develop a hypothesis—a possible answer to the question—and then set about testing the hypothesis to see whether it is right or wrong. When scientists discover that a hypothesis is wrong, they may be disappointed, but they move on to a new hypothesis, having gained valuable information from being wrong.

"Let the science speak."[2]

—Dr. Anthony Fauci, presidential adviser and director of the National Institute of Allergy and Infectious Diseases

In 2020 the process of science happened from day to day and was reported in the news as new patterns were identified and new evidence emerged. One of the clearest voices for science during the coronavirus pandemic was Dr. Anthony Fauci, presidential adviser and director of the National Institute of Allergy and Infectious Diseases. Fauci gave this simple advice on managing the coronavirus problem: "Let the science speak."[2]

CHAPTER ONE

The Coronavirus Circled the Globe

Not every germ or outbreak becomes a global pandemic. There are many factors that limit the spread of a contagious disease, but the COVID-19 pandemic was a perfect storm of contagion, even with all the scientific advancements and advantages available in the twenty-first century. In 2020 the coronavirus moved fast. Its spread was accelerated by global travel, close contact, and large gatherings of people. The coronavirus could travel in a human body, slipping undetected past every geographic boundary and national border. By the end of 2020, it had spread to every continent on earth.

From Asia to Antarctica in Less than a Year

From the city of Wuhan, the coronavirus first moved to other parts of China. It then appeared in Thailand, carried by a traveler who flew from Wuhan. Shortly thereafter, it spread across Asia, showing up in Nepal, Malaysia, Singapore, South Korea, Vietnam, Taiwan, India, and Japan. By the end of January 2020, it had reared its head in Europe, with cases in France and Germany, and in North America, as the United States identified its first cases. It struck Australia, carried by a traveler returning from China.

In February 2020 the coronavirus continued its spread through Asia, Europe, North America, and Australia. The first cases appeared in the Middle Eastern countries of Kuwait, Bahrain, Iraq, Oman, Qatar, and the United Arab Emirates. Israel reported its first case, brought home by a passenger on a cruise ship. In mid-February coronavirus hit the continent of Africa, as the first case was reported in Egypt. By the end of February, the number of infections worldwide had passed eighty-two thousand, including more than twenty-eight hundred deaths.

The coronavirus was found in South America near the end of February, when Brazil confirmed its first case. In early March 2020 Saudi Arabia announced its first coronavirus cases, as did Turkey, Ivory Coast, Honduras, Bolivia, Democratic Republic of the Congo, Panama, and Mongolia. The coronavirus was spreading swiftly through Asia, Europe, North America, Australia, Africa, and South America, sickening and killing people wherever it went. In December 2020, when cases of COVID-19 were reported at a research station in Antarctica, the coronavirus had reached every continent on earth.

Why Did It Spread So Fast?

There were many reasons for the rapid spread of coronavirus, some of which were not well understood early in the pandemic. Global travel, airborne transmission, and asymptomatic spread were among the biggest reasons the coronavirus easily made its way through the human population.

Air travel contributed to the wide and rapid spread of the coronavirus. On passenger airplanes, large numbers of people routinely travel long distances very quickly. The emergence of the coronavirus at the end of 2019 coincided with the start of a busy travel season in China. Much of the early spread of the coronavirus happened in January, carried by millions who traveled to visit friends and family for the lunar new year holiday.

A similar wave of travel and spread occurred in the United States two months later in March 2020, when large numbers of

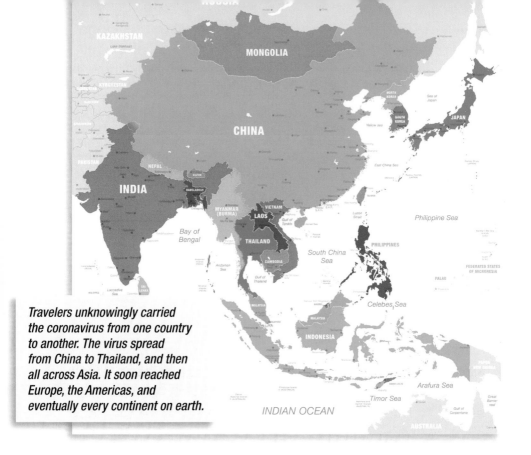

Travelers unknowingly carried the coronavirus from one country to another. The virus spread from China to Thailand, and then all across Asia. It soon reached Europe, the Americas, and eventually every continent on earth.

students traveled to beaches and resorts for spring break, carrying the coronavirus with them. People knew about the coronavirus, but in the beginning many were reluctant to adapt to the new pandemic reality. As one American college student remarked on a beach in Miami, Florida, "If I get corona, I get corona. At the end of the day, I'm not gonna let it stop me from partying."[3] At the time, the United States had no domestic travel restrictions, and only 150 people in the United States had died from COVID-19. Things would change very quickly, and the student later apologized publicly for the thoughtless remark. Before travel restrictions went into effect, the coronavirus had hitched rides around the world, following long-standing travel traditions and patterns.

Within communities, the coronavirus moved from one person to another through close contact. The spread happened in places where people gathered and shared air in close proximity: in train and subway stations, elevators, cafeterias, and public restrooms. People who lived, worked, traveled, worshipped, and celebrated in close proximity to others were catching and spreading the coronavirus. As evidence accumulated over 2020, scientists realized that coronavirus spread was much more likely to occur indoors, in a closed environment, than outdoors. The coronavirus spread in bars, restaurants, and shopping centers; it spread at concerts and sporting events. Spread occurred at weddings, funerals, parties, religious services, exercise classes, workplaces, prisons, and of course, hospitals, doctor's offices, and nursing homes.

> "If I get corona, I get corona. At the end of the day, I'm not gonna let it stop me from partying."[3]
>
> —American college student on spring break

Coronavirus in the Air

Controlling a disease requires understanding it, and in early 2020 scientists did not yet fully understand COVID-19. Some similar illnesses, such as SARS and influenza, spread when the body expels germ-laden droplets through coughing and sneezing. But the new coronavirus was spreading through smaller aerosolized droplets. The drops were so tiny that they stayed airborne and moved readily through the air, unlike the larger drops expelled by sneezing. In weather terms, the aerosolized droplets were more like mist than raindrops. Even normal speech expelled the tiny drops. Yelling, singing, and exercising together also contributed to the spread.

One person with the coronavirus infected two to three other people, on average, but the coronavirus spread to many more people during "super-spreader" events. In March 2020 a choir rehearsal in Mount Vernon, Washington, showed scientists in the United States how readily the coronavirus was spreading.

At the rehearsal of the Skagit Valley Chorale, singers gathered and sang for just over two hours. One singer recalled that the event seemed like a normal rehearsal—nobody was coughing and nobody seemed sick. Over the weeks that followed, fifty-three of the sixty-one people who had attended the rehearsal were infected with COVID-19, and two died. Choir member Carolynn Comstock expressed shock and sorrow at the loss of her friends. "It's just normal random people doing things that they love to do, and all of a sudden some people are dead," she said. "It's very sobering."[4]

Health officials concluded that the coronavirus had spread through the air from one singer to many. The act of singing likely spread the coronavirus. Singing together in groups—a normal thing that people often do—came to be considered high risk during the coronavirus pandemic.

Asymptomatic and Exponential Spread

The coronavirus was super contagious because it could spread undetected from person to person. The incubation period—the amount of time between exposure to the coronavirus and the first symptoms—was usually about five or six days. Seemingly healthy people walked around for days, unaware that they were spreading the coronavirus, before falling ill. Others—one-third to one-half of infected people—carried and spread the coronavirus but did not get sick at all. The spread was invisible at first, but later in the cycle of disease, COVID-19 became visible in a terrible way, when hospitals were overwhelmed with sick and dying people.

The spread of the coronavirus from one contagious person to two or three other people was far worse than it seemed at first. Many people imagined, incorrectly, that the disease moved through the population in a gradual, linear way, as a long chain of infection circling the globe. This misunderstanding existed even among educated populations. "People mistakenly perceive the coronavirus to grow in a linear manner, underestimating its actual potential for exponential growth,"[5] states a study by the National Academy of Sciences.

The Basketball Bubble

Controlling the spread of the coronavirus was difficult even in the best circumstances, and most efforts were only partially successful. In the United States the National Basketball Association (NBA) succeeded in keeping the coronavirus away from its players and staff by creating the "NBA bubble." This was a complex of buildings near Orlando, Florida, where teams lived, trained, and played for several months. Eight regular-season games and the 2020 play-offs were played inside the NBA bubble. The games were televised but without spectators.

Some players missed their families and found life in the bubble difficult. When asked about his experience, basketball star LeBron James said, "It's probably been the most challenging thing I've ever done as far as a professional." The experiment was a success. The basketball season ended in October without a single case of COVID-19 in the NBA bubble.

Quoted in Melissa Rohlin, "LeBron James Has Survived 82 Days in the Bubble by Focusing on Winning a Championship," *Sports Illustrated*, September 29, 2020. www.si.com.

The spread of COVID-19 was not linear; it was exponential. Exponential spread happens invisibly at first and then emerges in bursts, overwhelming all the medical resources, in what scientists and mathematicians call an exponential curve. On a graph the exponential curve is not a gradual slope. It takes a sudden, steep turn and lurches upward. If each person infects three others, three cases become sixty thousand cases in a very short time. The exponential curve became an important part of public health communication during 2020 in the efforts to slow the spread of the coronavirus.

Slowing the Spread

The fight against the coronavirus was a gigantic global mobilization, but it had a slow start. In the very early days, public health officials in China believed they had contained the spread by shutting down the seafood market in Wuhan that was connected to some of the cases. On January 23 the WHO declared that there was "no evidence"[6] of the coronavirus spreading between humans outside of China. The delay in recognizing and releasing information about human-to-human transmission resulted in a loss of valuable time. The coronavirus had a head start.

Seven days later, on January 30, the WHO director-general Tedros Adhanom Ghebreyesus acknowledged human-to-human transmission and changed the message of the WHO: "The only way we will defeat this outbreak is for all countries to work together in a spirit of solidarity and cooperation. We are all in this together, and we can only stop it together. This is the time for facts, not fear. This is the time for science, not rumours. This is the time for solidarity, not stigma."[7]

> "We are all in this together, and we can only stop it together."[7]
>
> —Tedros Adhanom Ghebreyesus, WHO director-general

Efforts to stop the coronavirus did not succeed in 2020. On December 31, 2020, the Johns Hopkins Coronavirus Resource Center recorded these sobering statistics: on a global scale, 83.3 million cases of infection and 1.8 million deaths; in the United States, 19.9 million cases of infection and more than 345,000 deaths. Efforts to slow down the virus's spread eventually had some success. But that success came only after many thousands more had died.

Flattening the Curve

Scientists rightly predicted that the spread of the coronavirus would be exponential, and they warned the public that hospitals could soon be flooded with sick and dying people. If health care systems were overwhelmed, the suffering could be terrible. The key to managing the pandemic was slowing the spread of the disease to allow health systems to care for sick patients without being overwhelmed and to give scientists time to develop COVID-19 treatments and vaccines.

Around the world, governments encouraged their populations to help flatten the curve—reduce the sharpness of that extreme exponential growth curve—and avoid a sudden flood of cases that could swamp their health care systems. To flatten the curve, many countries imposed restrictions to keep people from moving around and gathering. Travel was curtailed, and all but essential businesses were closed down. Science-based strategies were then used to control the spread. Those strategies included testing, quarantine, contact tracing, hand washing, face masks, and physical distancing.

One major strategy for slowing the spread was reducing the number of people who travel and the frequency of travel. Most countries around the world closed down all except essential travel. Some governments closed borders to nonresidents, banned flights from areas where the virus was spreading, or suspended international flights altogether.

Travel closer to home was also curtailed as stay-at-home orders were imposed. Many businesses were forced to close. Office workers stopped commuting to work, instead working from home. Likewise, children stayed home where possible and attended online school. Slowing the spread required curtailing many everyday activities and canceling public gatherings. Populations were generally discouraged from sharing indoor spaces.

Physical Distancing and Face Masks

Around the world, people were directed to follow simple rules to prevent the spread of the coronavirus: wash hands, wear a face mask over the mouth and nose, and stay 6 feet (1.8 m) away from

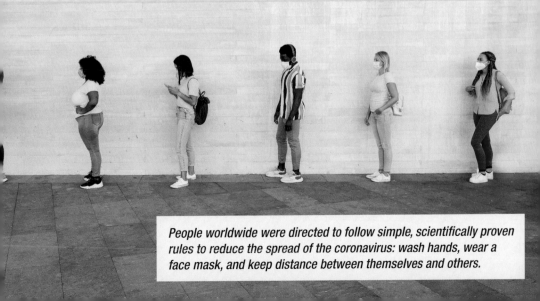

People worldwide were directed to follow simple, scientifically proven rules to reduce the spread of the coronavirus: wash hands, wear a face mask, and keep distance between themselves and others.

other people. Scientific studies had proved that these actions were effective in reducing (though not eliminating) the spread of disease. In a short time masks became ubiquitous in public places around the world. In many places, mask wearing was mandated by governments and required by businesses, and although it was well supported by the science, it was oddly controversial.

Backlash against public health restrictions and refusal to comply exacerbated the spread of coronavirus in some places, particularly in the United States, where mask requirements were rejected by some as too restrictive of personal freedom. "Making individual decisions is the American way," said Max Parsell, a power company worker near Jacksonville, Florida. "I don't want the government telling me I have to wear a mask."[8]

But Jeremy Howard, a data scientist in California, joined a public call by scientists for masks to be mandatory nationwide. Howard compared face masks to pants. "Pretty much every state requires that you wear pants in public," he said. "A mask is much more important from a hygiene point of view. If you don't wear pants, you're probably not going to kill anybody. But if you're not going to wear a mask, you absolutely might kill people."[9]

Testing, Contact Tracing, and Quarantine

Like masks and physical distance, some of the other public health strategies used to contain the coronavirus were similarly simple and time tested. Testing, contact tracing, and quarantines were not universally successful in 2020, but public health experts have noted that they probably reduced the spread in some places.

Early in the pandemic, if medical tests for the coronavirus had been available in large quantities, widespread testing might have been effective in slowing the spread. But developing and manufacturing scientific tests takes time, and again the coronavirus had a head start. When tests became available, they provided useful information for managing the spread. In places with high rates of positive tests, shutdowns were imposed. People who tested positive were told to quarantine. Through contact trac-

Coronavirus from Bats?

After the emergence of SARS-CoV-2, the coronavirus that causes COVID-19, scientists knew where to search for its origins. A similar coronavirus, the one that caused SARS in 2003, had originated in bats in China. Researchers soon found DNA evidence that a coronavirus carried by horseshoe bats near Wuhan, China, was closely related to SARS-COV-2. Scientific evidence seemed to support the theory that the coronavirus passed to humans from bats and other animals, possibly pangolins—also known as scaly anteaters. People were likely exposed to the coronavirus at markets where wild animals were sold for food. The origin of the coronavirus was not proved in 2020, but scientists recognized that transmission of disease from animals to humans would require study and vigilant monitoring in order to prevent future pandemics.

ing, potential carriers of the coronavirus were identified and also placed under quarantine.

The strategy of quarantine to manage infectious disease is thousands of years old. Quarantine slows the spread of coronavirus by separating people with potential exposure to the virus from the rest of the population. In 2020 testing improved the effectiveness of this ancient strategy.

Testing, tracing, and quarantine strategies worked best in isolated or controlled environments with plenty of funding. Some professional sports leagues, universities, Hollywood and Bollywood film production sets, research stations in Antarctica, and the island nation of New Zealand were successful in nearly eliminating the spread of the coronavirus through testing, tracing, and quarantine. But in most parts of the world, these strategies were too little, too late.

A Tiny Town That Stopped the Spread

Early in the pandemic a tiny town in northeastern Italy proved that testing, with coordinated quarantine and shutdown, could be effective in stopping the coronavirus. Vo is an isolated community, surrounded by farmland and vineyards. When the coronavirus mysteriously arrived, residents were shocked. On February 21 a resident of Vo, a retired roofer in his seventies, died of COVID-19. Nobody knew how he could have been exposed to the coronavirus. He had no contact, direct or indirect, to any traveler from China. But the coronavirus had come to Vo, and the local, regional, and national government mobilized to respond.

Italian soldiers were sent to close the roads to Vo, and no one could enter or leave. Food and medicine were brought in for the residents, who were directed to stay at home. Local health officials quickly administered coronavirus tests to everyone in town, and all those who tested positive were placed under strict, monitored quarantine.

The strategy worked in Vo: two weeks later a second round of testing found no new cases. "Lock down the village, test everybody, and isolate the positives," said virologist Andrea Crisanti, who directed the effort in Vo. "It really works."[10] However, Crisanti's strategy for stopping the spread was only effective when

A medical professional works with a COVID-19 patient in a hospital intensive care unit in November 2020 in Bergamo, Italy. One tiny town in northeastern Italy managed to stop the virus's spread but the rest of the country did not fare as well.

the problem was small, in isolated areas with abundant resources for testing. On a larger scale, it would have required a massive mobilization of public health resources. Italy did not succeed in stopping the spread throughout the rest of the country. Later that spring, Italy had one of the severest outbreaks in the world, followed by a surge again in the fall. And scientists never figured out how the coronavirus came to Vo.

Relentless Waves and Spikes

Despite efforts to slow the spread around the world, the coronavirus did spread, and in many places where it was brought under control, it surged again. Spread accelerated with seasons and travel, slowed again with prevention measures, and often surged again as people became impatient and began to defy public health restrictions. People around the world grew frustrated with wearing masks and discouraged by news that a vaccine would likely take years to develop.

After a terrible spring season in 2020, most European countries had control of the coronavirus by summer. Still, the coronavirus surged again and receded again as public health restrictions were relaxed and then tightened again. The United States experienced a surge every season, with different regions suffering at different times. The cities were hit hard early and rural areas later. North and South America were the worst-struck regions in the world, in terms of case count and fatalities, but Asia and Europe were not far behind.

The coronavirus reshaped the world in 2020. What began as a mysterious illness in Wuhan, China, spread in an exponential growth pattern across all seven continents of the globe. By the end of 2020 the Johns Hopkins University Coronavirus Resource Center had tallied 83.3 million coronavirus infections worldwide and a global COVID-19 death toll of 1.8 million.

CHAPTER TWO

A Year of Pandemic Suffering

Few people on earth were unaffected by the coronavirus pandemic of 2020. The toll was gradual at first, rising and striking in waves till few places were left unscarred. Hundreds of millions of people were infected, and millions died. Lives were suddenly and dramatically changed. As the coronavirus spread, people everywhere began to worry—for their health, their friends and family members, their jobs, their businesses, and their futures. The coronavirus pandemic overwhelmed health care systems, collapsed economies, and devastated families. It was a year of suffering—death, sickness, loss, upended lives, and isolation—for people all over the world.

The severity of the illness caught many people by surprise. Survival and recovery were cause for celebration. In March 2020 fifty-six-year-old Theirrien Clark was not feeling well. He had a low fever and a cough but was otherwise in good health, so there was no reason for alarm. But the cough did not improve, and he began to have trouble breathing. In the emergency room his chest X-ray showed signs of COVID-19 lung damage. Doctors connected Clark to a ventilator, a machine to help him breathe, and moved him to the intensive care unit (ICU). He spent four weeks in the ICU critically ill, battling COVID-19. He developed a dangerous excessive immune response known as a cytokine storm, in which his body began to attack itself rather than just the virus. Clark came very close to dying, but he survived.

Gradually, Clark began to recover enough that the breathing tube could be removed. When he left the ICU after twenty-eight days on a ventilator, doctors and nurses in the hallway turned and applauded as he wheeled by. "It was so emotional when they were clapping for me," Clark said. "Most people as sick as I was don't make it."[11] Clark had not seen his family in weeks, and he had to relearn how to walk and to eat and drink without choking. He had spent forty-six days in the hospital and had months of recovery ahead. Still, he was a COVID-19 survivor.

> "Most people as sick as I was don't make it."[11]
>
> —Theirrien Clark, COVID-19 survivor

Some Suffered and Others Were Spared

The suffering from the disease itself varied widely. Many people who were infected with the coronavirus never knew they had it. Others seemed to defeat it easily in two weeks or less, experiencing only a mild respiratory illness similar to the flu. But some cases that seemed mild at first turned suddenly severe, as people woke in the night unable to breath and were rushed to the hospital. Scientists estimated that about one person died for every one hundred infections worldwide. Of those who developed symptoms, 5 percent suffered critical, potentially deadly symptoms, 14 percent developed severe symptoms, and 81 percent developed mild to moderate symptoms.

Older people were more likely to have severe symptoms and far more likely to die of COVID-19. Advanced age was the greatest risk factor, but people with other health vulnerabilities—such as cancer, obesity, heart conditions, and chronic illness—were also at high risk.

In most severe cases, the coronavirus staged a ferocious attack on the lungs, and many of those who survived COVID-19 suffered permanent lung damage. It attacked more than the lungs, though. As cases of COVID-19 were studied over the first year of the pandemic, researchers found that the coronavirus infected many parts of the body, including the brain, heart, blood vessels, kidneys, liver, and intestines. It was a complicated and dangerous disease.

One dangerous symptom of COVID-19 that occurred in some adults was a clotting syndrome in the circulatory system. This syndrome caused multiple strokes, leading to death for some people and permanent damage in others. Abnormal blood clotting from COVID-19 was found in many organs in people who developed this syndrome. "Autopsies have shown some people's lungs fill with hundreds of microclots,"[12] according to *Washington Post* reporter Ariana Eunjung Cha.

In about 30 percent of severe cases, patients had abnormal blood clotting in multiple organs, which sometimes led to multiple organ failure and death. Among those who contracted the coro-

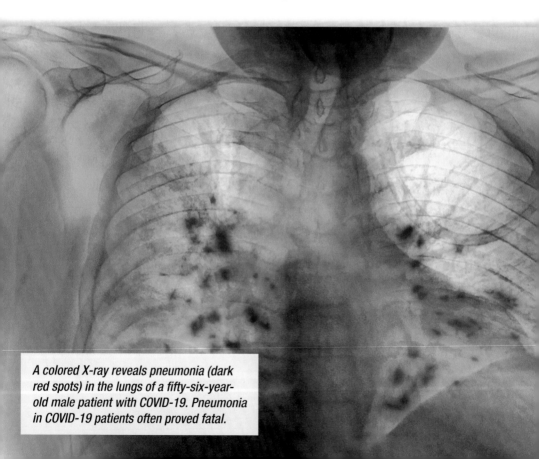

A colored X-ray reveals pneumonia (dark red spots) in the lungs of a fifty-six-year-old male patient with COVID-19. Pneumonia in COVID-19 patients often proved fatal.

navirus and then developed blood clots was forty-one-year-old Broadway actor Nick Cordero. According to Cha, Cordero "had his right leg amputated after being infected with the novel coronavirus and suffering from clots that blocked blood from getting to his toes."[13] He died in July 2020, three months after being hospitalized with COVID-19.

Overwhelmed Health Care Workers

During the COVID-19 spikes that happened around the world, at different times in different places, hospitals were overwhelmed, flooded with more COVID-19 cases than they could safely handle. Emergency rooms and hallways were filled with patients. In big cities around the world, ambulances carrying COVID-19 patients waited and circled outside hospitals that were too full to take more patients. Hospitals ran out of rooms and beds, patients were kept on gurneys in hallways, and nurses had more patients than they could possibly care for. Patients were moved to medical facilities that still had room, but those soon filled up and were also overwhelmed.

Health care systems were "on the edge of breaking" in 2020, according to Michael Osterholm, a prominent US epidemiologist. Osterholm described patients in the United States who were "sitting in chairs in waiting rooms in emergency rooms for 10 hours to get a bed, and they can't find one, and then they die."[14]

The pandemic took a harsh toll on health care workers and support staff—from the doctors, nurses, and respiratory therapists to the workers who cleaned hospital buildings. Caring for patients with COVID-19 was a dangerous job. More than twenty-nine hundred US health care workers contracted COVID-19 and died from March to December 2020, according to a report from Kaiser Health News and the *Guardian*, a British newspaper.

Alfredo and Susana Pabatao were both health care workers on the front lines of the coronavirus pandemic. Alfredo worked as an orderly—a patient transporter—in a medical center in North Bergen, New Jersey, and Susana was a nursing assistant at a nursing home. The couple, who were US citizens, had immigrated to the United States with their children in 2001 from Quezon City, Philippines.

At age sixty-eight, Alfredo had worked at the hospital for nearly twenty years. In March 2020 Alfredo became ill, just a few days after transporting a patient who had COVID-19 symptoms. Susana also became ill, and both were hospitalized. Alfredo and Susana died within a week of each other at the end of March 2020, in the hospital where Alfredo had worked. They had been married for forty-four years. Because of the hospital's COVID-19 restrictions, the two died alone, on separate floors, away from their children.

Constant Risk

Health care workers who survived the coronavirus and remained on the job in 2020 suffered relentless loss, stress, exhaustion, and sadness. They faced the constant risk of infection when protective equipment like masks, gloves, gowns, and face shields were in short supply. Workers themselves were also in short supply—some got sick and others had to be quarantined after exposure to the coronavirus—compounding the burden for those who were still at work.

At Livingstone Hospital, a designated COVID-19 hospital in Port Elizabeth, South Africa, the suffering of the pandemic was intensified by a fragile, underfunded health system, with a shortage of nurses and a lack of medical supplies and protective equipment. Conditions in the hospital were not sanitary, and staff were not protected against infection. Visitors to Livingstone Hospital during the pandemic reported blood and waste on the floors, and newspaper, rather than sheets and blankets, used to cover sleeping patients.

Some workers became sick with COVID-19, and others quit, troubled by the working conditions and afraid of infection. The staff who stayed worked double and triple shifts. Doctors did the hospital laundry and nurses cleaned and cooked for patients, in

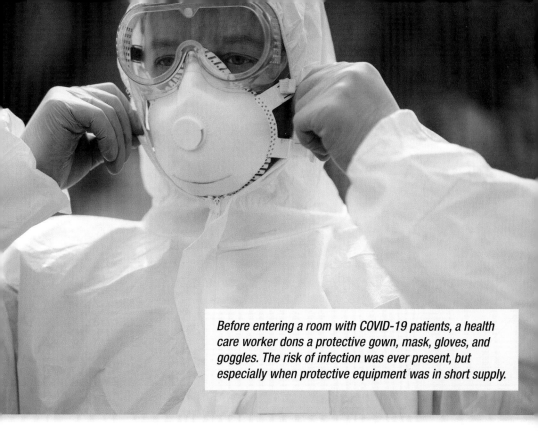

Before entering a room with COVID-19 patients, a health care worker dons a protective gown, mask, gloves, and goggles. The risk of infection was ever present, but especially when protective equipment was in short supply.

addition to their other work. The situation was unsustainable, and burnout was inevitable. Khaya Sodidi, head of the nurses' union in South Africa, said, "Our nurses are overwhelmed, having to clean floors or cook because kitchen staff are not working. We cannot risk the lives of nurses."[15] It was not until the central government of South Africa dispatched a military planeload of army medics to Livingstone Hospital that conditions finally improved.

> "We cannot risk the lives of nurses."[15]
>
> —Khaya Sodidi, head of the nurses' union in South Africa

Ripples of Suffering

Throughout the world, the millions of COVID-19 deaths caused ripples of suffering that extended to many millions of people. Fear played a terrible role in the suffering. In Venezuela, a woman died after she likely delayed treatment because she was afraid to tell her family about her COVID-19 diagnosis. Verónica García

Many of the deadliest complications of COVID-19 were due to a phenomenon called a cytokine storm, which causes a patient's immune system to malfunction. Cytokine storms are not unique to COVID-19; they also occur in other diseases. But in 2020 they were linked to many of the COVID-19 deaths.

Cytokine proteins are usually a beneficial part of the body's immune response, but when a cytokine storm occurs, the immune system goes haywire and begins to attack healthy tissue. In response to coronavirus infection, the immune system floods the body, particularly the lungs, with an excess of cytokines, which break down the lung tissues. The lungs fill with fluid, causing difficulty breathing, pneumonia, and damage to the lungs. In the worst cases, the body is deprived of oxygen, resulting in organ failure and death.

As doctors came to recognize cytokine storms in COVID-19 patients, they established treatments and protocols to prevent such responses. By the end of 2020, the number of COVID-19 deaths due to cytokine storms had begun to decline.

Fuentes, age thirty-six, developed a fever in mid-December 2020. "She took a [COVID-19] test which came back positive and isolated herself at home, but she told her husband and children she had a bad case of the flu,"[16] according to *Newsweek* reporter Lydia Smith.

Fuentes's symptoms worsened, and she was admitted to a hospital, where she died of COVID-19. In the weeks that followed, sorrow turned to devastation in the Fuentes family, as her husband (age thirty-three) and three children (four-year-old twins and a seventeen-year-old) also fell ill and died of COVID-19.

Isolated and Alone

A heartbreaking but all-too-common story of suffering caused by the coronavirus was that many people died alone in the hospitals, without their families near for comfort, because hospitals could not allow visitors. Some families were able to stay in touch by phone or teleconference apps, but remote connection was difficult with a person who was on a ventilator or unconscious. Many health care workers recounted workdays in 2020 when they sat holding a dying patient's hand, just to offer some human contact in the final moments of life.

CNN reporter Daniel Burke wrote of a New York man who fell ill with COVID-19: "Steve Kaminski was whisked into an ambulance near his home on New York's Upper East Side. He never saw his family again. Kaminski died days later of covid-19, the disease caused by the novel coronavirus. Because of fears of contagion, no visitors, including his family, were allowed to see him at Mt. Sinai Hospital before he died."[17] The family was shocked and anguished that they could not be with their loved one as he died, but in 2020 there were countless stories like Kaminski's.

People in nursing homes and assisted living facilities also could not receive visits, because coronavirus was particularly deadly for the elderly and medically vulnerable. The isolation and loneliness in such facilities could be extreme, particularly with illness and death all around.

> "Steve Kaminski was whisked into an ambulance near his home on New York's Upper East Side. He never saw his family again."[17]
>
> —Daniel Burke, CNN reporter

As people heard and shared the many sad stories of COVID-19 in 2020, they felt afraid that the loss—loss of breath, loss of life, loss of job, loss of loved ones—would hit them next. People of all ages felt fear and hopelessness, and because of pandemic restrictions, it was difficult for families and friends to be together to comfort each other.

Anxiety and Depression Grow

The coronavirus pandemic affected mental health in many ways, particularly with widespread isolation that resulted from stay-at-home orders. Rates of addiction, anxiety, insomnia, and depression all increased during the pandemic. A study by the *Journal of the American Medical Association* found that cases of depression in the United States tripled over the course of the pandemic. Young adults, racial and ethnic minorities, and essential workers experienced disproportionately worse mental health conditions associated with the coronavirus pandemic, compared to the rest of the population.

Young people around the globe felt isolated, scared of getting sick, and worried about their parents and grandparents. Teenagers suffered at the separation from friends, at an age when friendships and relationships are central to their sense of belonging. Students had their lives disrupted when schools were closed and classes were taught remotely. Remote education meant separation from teachers and classmates. And teenagers and young adults missed out on sports, graduations, summer jobs, parties, and trips. Stuck inside with their parents—or alone—many teenagers felt depressed, lonely, and bored.

Separated from friends and missing out on sports, graduations, summer jobs, parties, and other activities, many teenagers experienced depression. Disrupted school schedules also led to heightened anxiety among students.

Long COVID

Many survivors of COVID-19 developed "long-haul" health effects after recovery, including extreme fatigue, muscle weakness, trouble sleeping, and problems with concentration and thinking. Some people continued to experience a range of effects—also known as long COVID—for many months after recovery. A 2020 study of people who had recovered from COVID-19 in Wuhan, China, showed that six months later 76 percent of patients had at least one symptom of long COVID, including psychological aftereffects such as anxiety and depression. In their study findings, the researchers noted, "At 6 months after symptom onset, fatigue or muscle weakness and sleep difficulties were the main symptoms of patients who had recovered from COVID-19. Risk of anxiety or depression as an important psychological complication and impaired pulmonary diffusion capacities were higher in patients with more severe illness."

Chaolin Huang et al., "6-Month Consequences of COVID-19 in Patients Discharged from Hospital: A Cohort Study," *The Lancet*, January 8, 2021. www.thelancet.com.

A nationwide US study released in March 2021 revealed that rates of depression among young people had increased during the pandemic. Thirty-eight percent of teenagers and young adults reported moderate to severe depression (compared with 25 percent two years earlier). And depression rates were much higher among young people whose friends and families were directly affected by coronavirus infection.

A Year of Suffering Comes to a Close

As 2020 ended, North America and South America combined had more than 50 percent of all reported coronavirus deaths, and Europe and Asia were not far behind. The United States, by far the worst-affected country in the world, had seen its deadliest year in history. The suffering went on as the coronavirus continued its rampage of sickness and death around the globe. Health care workers were exhausted. It had been a year of suffering, and many people had lost family and friends to COVID-19. People around the world desperately hoped for better in the year to come.

CHAPTER THREE

Pandemic Shock to the Global Economy

The sickness, suffering, and death caused by the pandemic also brought about widespread economic disruption and hardship. The response by governments was equally damaging. When news of the coronavirus emerged, the first priority of countries around the world was to prevent the spread. Governments issued stay-at-home orders and imposed shutdowns. Some countries closed borders, restricted travel, ordered mandatory quarantines, and set curfews. In the long term, preventing the spread reduced the damage to the global economy, but in the short term, these actions caused enormous economic pain.

When any sweeping change happens in the world, the effects are felt in the economy. In 2020 the shutdown of industry, commerce, and consumer spending happened suddenly. Worldwide economic activity contracted sharply. Enormous change happened in a short span of time, and the result was economic shock.

The contraction of economic activity was not only imposed by governments. Many businesses voluntarily closed stores, offices, and factories to protect the health and safety of their customers and workers. People worldwide sharply reduced shopping, travel, and social activity for their own health and safety and that of their family members and friends. Individuals, businesses, and governments changed how they operated, and the economy stopped growing.

Economists use global gross domestic product (GDP)—the value of all the goods and services produced in the world—to track the size of the global economy. In healthy economic times, the global GDP grows by 2–3 percent per year. In 2020, the economy not only stopped growing—it started shrinking. According to the International Monetary Fund, by the end of 2020, the global economy had shrunk by about 4.4 percent as a result of the pandemic.

Global Financial Markets Crashed

The economic shock and uncertainty of the pandemic caused trouble in the global financial markets. When a large number of investors—those who have money in the stock markets—start to panic and try to get their money out of the market, a crash can be the result. Prices of stocks plummet, causing investments to lose their value. A series of such crashes, including the steepest

Midtown Manhattan in New York City is ghostly quiet during a government-imposed lockdown in 2020. Stay-at-home orders and shutdowns helped slow the spread of the virus, but these actions also caused enormous economic pain.

in more than thirty years, happened in late February and March 2020 as a result of the pandemic. The crashes in turn triggered the largest worldwide recession in history and the most severe global economic crisis since the Great Depression of the 1930s.

The concept of supply and demand is often used to explain what happens in the economy. People and companies supply goods and services by making things, like soccer balls, or providing services, like cleaning office buildings, for money. And people and companies demand goods and services by buying things like soccer balls or paying a cleaning company to clean a building.

During the coronavirus pandemic of 2020, both supply and demand were disrupted. People and companies closed factories and stopped making soccer balls, and cleaning companies kept their workers at home. Meanwhile, the demand for soccer balls and cleaning services dropped, when stores, soccer leagues, and office buildings shut down. "Supply and demand" describes these essential buying and selling economic activities, but many other factors play a role in the economy and are affected by change. For example, workers earn wages and spend money on food and housing. The coronavirus pandemic disrupted simply everything, all over the globe.

The pandemic began in China at a time in history when much of the world was dependent on Chinese manufacturing. In early 2020, when factories in China were forced to close, supplies of many types of goods were disrupted. At the same time, demand was increasing sharply for certain manufactured goods, particularly medical supplies and protective equipment. For example, hospitals all over the world were desperately trying to buy surgical masks but could not find an adequate supply.

Shortages and Panic Buying

When the demand for all sorts of goods exceeded the supply, shortages occurred. When shortages occurred, panic buying and hoarding also occurred, making matters worse. In many places, food market shelves could not be stocked fast enough, as shoppers stockpiled nonperishable food. One of the strangest stories of 2020 was the worldwide panic buying of toilet paper, driven by rumors on social media of a shortage that did not actually exist. The panic buying then caused real shortages in some areas, although these shortages were temporary.

As early as February, for instance, Hong Kong experienced a shortage of toilet paper. As a reporter for the Hong Kong Free Press news website wrote, "Panic buyers in Hong Kong have descended on supermarkets to snap up toilet rolls as the government warned that online rumours of shortages were hampering the city's fight against a deadly coronavirus outbreak. Videos . . . showed long queues of frantic shoppers packing trolleys with multiple packets of toilet rolls, with some arguments breaking out."[18]

> "Panic buyers in Hong Kong have descended on supermarkets to snap up toilet rolls as the government warned that online rumours of shortages were hampering the city's fight against a deadly coronavirus outbreak."[18]
>
> —Reporter, Hong Kong Free Press

A shopper at a Costco in San Francisco loads up on toilet paper early in the pandemic. Most stores eventually imposed limits on the purchase of toilet paper and some other products after panic buying led to major shortages.

Job Losses

Unemployment was part of the huge, sudden shock of the global recession. When businesses closed, people lost their jobs, creating a downward economic spiral. People who lost jobs reduced their spending, reducing the income of the businesses they bought from, and so on.

In India, the shutdown of cities caused a sudden massive wave of homelessness, as millions of migrant workers lost their jobs. Many of these workers could no longer afford food and shelter. "Some of us will die, some of us will live to suffer," said Zakir Hussain, a worker in Delhi. "We are poor. We've been left here to die. Our lives are of no value to anyone."[19]

The pandemic affected different types of workers in different ways. Some workers, particularly office workers, were able to keep their jobs, working from home over computer networks. Remote work saved many jobs and in some countries helped sustain the economy through the pandemic.

But jobs that require in-person contact with other people could not be done remotely. Workers in food processing plants and factories and those who faced the public, as in grocery stores and public transportation, were essential to keep each country running. Workers in service jobs—in restaurants, hotels, personal care, and entertainment, for example—had little protection against layoffs and job cuts. Because of the nature of their jobs, they were vulnerable to catching the coronavirus, and they became infected in large numbers. Many died, and many suffered severe stress. Younger workers, women, and low-wage workers suffered more than other categories of workers, and typically they were also the least prepared economically to withstand the pandemic.

Without jobs, workers had trouble paying for food and shelter. In the United States long lines of cars waited at food banks, which

> "We are poor. We've been left here to die. Our lives are of no value to anyone."[19]
>
> —Zakir Hussain, worker in Delhi, India

The global film industry lost billions of dollars at the start of the pandemic, when movie theaters closed and film productions shut down. Bollywood, the large film industry based in Mumbai, India, took a severe economic hit. Bollywood movies, which often involve crowd scenes and large groups of dancers, were impossible to shoot under pandemic restrictions. Filmmakers had to figure out how to produce films under new conditions. Stories were adapted so that they could be filmed with smaller production teams, and strict protocols and quarantines were imposed so that filming could resume. Film producers devised ways to protect their cast and crew members from coronavirus infection. Many of these methods had no medical or scientific foundation. The *Los Angeles Times* described one such effort: "Among the most elaborate [protocols] are sprinkler systems that douse costumes in disinfectant and unproven sterilization rooms that apply ultraviolet light to camera kits and crew members."

Tish Sanghera, "Smaller Dance Sequences, Humbler Locations: How Bollywood Is Adapting to COVID-19," *Los Angeles Times*, November 20, 2020. www.latimes.com.

were inundated by people who needed food even as donations were dwindling. In regions of high poverty around the world, the pandemic made the existing problems worse. Poor living conditions, overcrowding, malnutrition, and inadequate sanitation compounded the suffering from COVID-19.

Tourism and Travel Were Hit Hard

In the interconnected web of economic activity worldwide, every economic sector affects every other. All sectors of the global economy were affected by the coronavirus pandemic of 2020. Among the hardest hit were the tourism, travel, and the oil and gas industries.

The coronavirus pandemic caused serious damage to the tourism and travel industries. When governments imposed stay-at-home orders, travel restrictions, and limitations on gatherings, many events all over the world were canceled. Conferences, concerts, religious gatherings, and sporting events, including the

Tokyo Summer Olympics, were canceled. Business and vacation trips were canceled. Museums, resorts, historical sites, and other tourist attractions were shut down. Shutdowns happened on an unprecedented scale. As a result, businesses faltered and failed, and millions of people lost their jobs, at least temporarily.

The pandemic-driven recession took a heavy toll on tourism in Egypt, for example, where 10 percent of workers have jobs in the tourism industry. Ashraf Nasr was a small business owner providing camel rides for tourists near the pyramids at Giza. Nasr had to sell two of his camels because he could not afford to feed them. "It's been so hard for everyone," said Nasr after four months without work due to the pandemic. "Each camel needs 100 Egyptian pounds [$6.00] a day for food."[20] Shahenda Adel, a tour guide, also had a hard year in 2020. "After the coronavirus, everything just disappeared,"[21] she said.

> "After the coronavirus, everything just disappeared."[21]
>
> —Shahenda Adel, tour guide in Giza, Egypt

As travelers canceled their travel plans, airlines canceled millions of flights. Air travel dropped 66 percent in 2020, to levels not seen in many years. The pandemic hit the airline industry so hard that some airlines went bankrupt and others required government support to stay aloft. And in this industry, too, many people lost their jobs. Many commercial pilots, for example, went from prestigious, high-paying jobs to unemployment, furlough (mandatory temporary leave of absence), or retirement. As newly hired pilots without seniority lost their jobs, others lived with the uncertainty of furlough, and older pilots were asked to take early retirement. By the end of 2020, almost half of all airline pilots (47 percent) were either unemployed or on furlough, according to a worldwide airline industry survey.

Greg Harper, an airline captain with twenty-five years of experience flying for Qantas Airways in Australia, took a job at his local grocery store after he and eighty-five hundred other Qantas employees were placed on furlough or lost their jobs. At age fifty-

The Business of Zoom

One of the rare businesses that profited and grew under pandemic conditions was a videoconference app called Zoom. During the COVID-19 pandemic, Zoom became a vital part of business, when many offices shut down and employees began to work remotely. Zoom was easy to use and widely available with internet access. Workers could work from anywhere, and business meetings were almost as easy to hold on Zoom as in person. In April 2020 Zoom's chief executive officer, Eric Yuan, reported that more than 200 million people were using Zoom every day.

Zoom's business strategy of focusing on only one product—the videoconference software—proved successful. According to NPR reporter Shannon Bond, "Zoom has emerged as one of the biggest corporate success stories of this year, as video meetings have become an essential part of work, school and entertainment for many people during the pandemic."

Shannon Bond, "Zoom Turns Record Profit Thanks to Coronavirus Shutdowns," NPR, August 31, 2020. www.npr.org.

two, Harper admitted to "feeling a bit silly cleaning shopping baskets,"[22] but he had a growing family to support. The four hundred thousand jobs lost in airlines worldwide included pilots and cabin crew. Workers who did not lose their jobs worked in confined, inside spaces with travelers from around the world—conditions that were newly hazardous because of the coronavirus.

Energy Industry Suffered Severe Shock

In 2020 the world economy depended heavily on energy from oil and gas. When the pandemic hit, and factories shut down and travel was curtailed, the demand for fuel dropped abruptly. China, the top consumer of oil and gas in the world, was the first country to shut down its economic activity. Oil refineries were stuck with unused barrels of oil, and the price of oil went into a freefall. On April 20, 2020, the price of oil in the US market did something weird: it temporarily dropped below zero. Oil producers had run out of storage for the excess supply and were forced to pay for storage. For a brief moment, the price of oil was less than nothing.

Before the pandemic, the International Energy Agency had projected that the worldwide demand for oil in 2020 would increase by eight hundred thousand barrels compared to 2019. After the pandemic hit, the agency revised its projection: instead, the worldwide demand for oil in 2020 would decrease by ninety thousand barrels compared to 2019.

The shock to the oil market caused repercussions all around the world. Many oil-producing companies were in wealthy countries that could weather an economic downturn, but in developing countries where oil was a primary source of national revenue, like Iraq, Venezuela, and Nigeria, the economic damage from the oil shock was especially severe. The loss of income and employment in those countries created dangerous conditions—worsening poverty and political instability—in the midst of the pandemic.

The conditions that created the oil shock did have one unexpected positive effect: less burning of oil and gas. Experts noted a decrease in carbon pollution in the atmosphere. The change marked a temporary reprieve for the global environment.

Restaurant and Food Service Industries Were Devastated

The restaurant industry suffered some of the most extreme losses from the pandemic. Many restaurants, bars, cafeterias, caterers, and other food service businesses were shut down to protect both customers and staff from COVID-19. According to the National Restaurant Association, more than 110,000 restaurants in the United States—one in six—closed permanently by the end of 2020. People who worked in restaurants—making food, waiting tables, cleaning, and running the business, lost their jobs and income.

Bettina Stern, co-owner of two vegetarian taco restaurants in Washington, DC, had thirty employees before the pandemic. The restaurants' sales dropped more than 80 percent because of the pandemic, and by the end of 2020, she had only two employees. However, Stern's business did survive, by switching quickly to

Workers clean up after COVID-19 restrictions forced their coffee shop to close. The restaurant industry suffered some of the most extreme losses from the pandemic.

take-out and delivery orders. "We limited our service hours, adopted a pared-down menu, and began serving customers exclusively through take-out and delivery," she told a reporter in May. "This helped us minimize employee exposure and reduce labor costs. We now operate with a two-person team that consists of one owner and one kitchen employee in each store."[23]

Many large fast-food restaurant chains already had a feature—the drive-through window—that helped them adapt to pandemic conditions. Drive-through ordering and pickup allows fast-food customers to buy food with very little contact. Although fast-food restaurants also suffered loss of sales due to the pandemic, they recovered more quickly than other types of restaurants. In an effort to quickly adapt to the pandemic conditions, some restaurants quickly added drive-through windows to their buildings and reconfigured their parking lots so they could sell food to drivers rather than diners.

Retail Continued an Ongoing Slide

The retail sector—which consists of malls, shopping centers, stores, and markets where people go to shop in person—had already been changing in the twenty-first century because of e-commerce. Shoppers were already buying things online. When the pandemic hit in 2020, whole populations curtailed their shopping, and retail businesses lost billions. Some retailers were able to survive by quickly shifting to e-commerce with delivery or curbside pickup. But others could not weather the change. Retail businesses around the world closed down, some temporarily and others permanently.

Most economic activity faltered or failed during the pandemic, but a few types of business flourished. Companies that sold essential goods like groceries and hardware, items that were necessary for everyday life, thrived. The demand remained strong for those goods during the pandemic.

E-commerce and delivery companies succeeded and even grew during the pandemic, because they allowed shoppers to buy what they needed without entering a physical store. Online shopping and delivery were needed more than they had been before the pandemic. Still, there were very few economic winners in 2020, and most of the economic news was grim. Help was needed, and many national governments took action.

Governments Stepped In to Help

Throughout the world, governments injected money into their national economies in various ways, in an effort to help workers, businesses, and municipalities survive the pandemic. To boost their national economies, central banks dropped interest rates, freeing up billions for banks to lend. Some governments devised paycheck protection programs, lending or granting money to businesses so they could keep paying their workers.

By the end of 2020, the global economic problems were serious and complicated. The shutdown of industry, commerce, and travel was followed by recession and unemployment. All this disruption, in the middle of an overwhelming health care crisis, was truly devastating to the world economy. People, businesses, and countries were affected in irreversible ways. The world had never before seen a truly global economic shutdown or such abrupt economic change.

CHAPTER FOUR

Vaccines to the Rescue

Throughout human history, certain infectious diseases have caused countless deaths and boundless suffering. Many of these very diseases were brought under control in modern times through vaccination. As the world was rocked by COVID-19 in 2020, scientists knew that the only way to control the coronavirus was by creating a vaccine and administering it to a large majority of the world's population. A coronavirus vaccine was desperately needed to slow the pandemic in 2020, but medical researchers and scientists predicted that it would take years to develop and even longer to deliver to billions of people. But through an enormous urgent international effort and plenty of human ingenuity, vaccines were developed astonishingly fast.

The Best Defense Against Coronavirus

When a new pathogen enters the human body, it creates an infection, invading cells and rapidly multiplying. The immune system uses its defenses—antibodies, or germ-fighting cells—to fight back. The battle against a pathogen may take days or weeks. If the germ is very new or very nasty, or if the body's immune system is not strong, the person may not survive. But if the immune system wins the battle and defeats the infection, it keeps its newly developed defensive weapons, the antibodies it developed to fight the pathogen. The next time the pathogen shows up, the immune system quickly defeats it. This happens all the time—the immune system defeats germs—but most germs are not as new or dangerous as the new coronavirus was in 2020.

Scientists began working on a shortcut to disease immunity in the 1700s. If they could help the body create immune defenses before the pathogen showed up, there would be no battle—or only a small battle—and the immune system would win. And if enough people had immune defenses, the disease would stop spreading.

To create this immunity and stop the spread of disease, scientists developed vaccines. A vaccine is a tiny inactive sample of a particular pathogen, or something that closely resembles the pathogen. The tiny sample cannot multiply, so it cannot become an infection. Vaccination of an individual—often by injection—stimulates the immune response that kills the pathogen. Vaccination uses the body's natural reaction to pathogens, but it is much safer than infection.

In 2020 different scientists used a variety of approaches, using parts of the new coronavirus to create the tiny inactive sample to use in a vaccine. Some of the vaccines used the virus itself—either killed or attenuated (weakened). The Sinovac vaccine, created by a Chinese company, was an attenuated-virus vaccine. The Sputnik V vaccine, developed by a Russian government research agency, was a viral-vector vaccine, using a common cold virus implanted with coronavirus spike proteins. Two other major partnerships also created viral-vector vaccines. One of these vaccines was developed by Johnson & Johnson, an American company, and Jansen, a Belgian-Dutch company. The other was developed by AstraZeneca, a Swedish-British company, and Oxford University in the United Kingdom.

Two of the most widely used vaccines were messenger RNA (mRNA) vaccines, which were created with genetic code from the new coronavirus. These RNA-based vaccines were predicted to be safer than the other types, but they had not been widely tested in humans. In addition, they were difficult to transport and store, since they had to be kept at very cold temperatures.

Immune System Defenses

The process of developing safe and effective vaccines begins with an understanding of the immune system's defenses. When a new pathogen enters the body, it creates an infection by invading the cells and rapidly multiplying. The human immune system fights this infection. It does this by making white blood cells which in turn produce Y-shaped molecules called antibodies. Antibodies can keep viruses from infecting the cells. But that protection may depend on where the antibody grips the virus and how tightly it holds on. This presented one of the key challenges to developing vaccines against COVID-19.

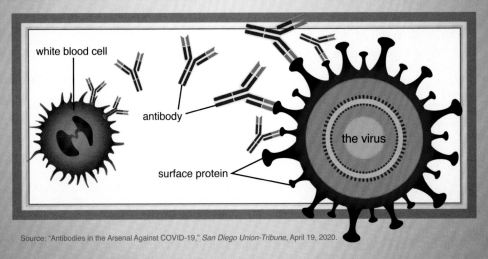

Source: "Antibodies in the Arsenal Against COVID-19," *San Diego Union-Tribune*, April 19, 2020.

Vaccine research and technology was already well developed in 2020, but adapting it to create a coronavirus vaccine for SARS-CoV-2, the coronavirus that causes COVID-19, would take time. Vaccine development takes ten to fifteen years on average. Before 2020 the fastest vaccine ever developed was the mumps vaccine, which was created and tested in four years. In addressing a group of scientists about the pandemic in February 2020, WHO director general Tedros Adhanom Ghebreyesus made a vaccine prediction that was widely considered to be overly optimistic: "The first vaccine could be ready in 18 months, so we have to do everything today using the available weapons to fight this virus, while preparing for the long-term."[24] The reality turned out to be better than his prediction.

Global Race to Create Coronavirus Vaccines

Lives and livelihoods depended on scientists creating a vaccine and ending the pandemic. A massive worldwide mobilization of resources was required to fund vaccine research, development, manufacturing, and distribution.

Private companies often compete in the creation of medicines and vaccines, and competition is believed to spur innovation. However, the coronavirus vaccine would require more than competition; it would require international cooperation—and that is what happened. Governments, nonprofit groups, universities, and private companies combined resources and worked together on vaccine research, to be done at a pace never before attempted. Tens of billions of dollars were invested to create dozens of vaccine candidates. Multiple competing vaccines would be completed on shortened timelines. According to Charles Schmidt of *Scientific American*:

> "The labs predicted that a commercial vaccine could be available for emergency or compassionate use by early 2021—incredibly fast, given that vaccines to brand-new pathogens have taken a decade to be perfected and deployed."[25]
>
> —Charles Schmidt, writer for *Scientific American*

By early April almost 80 companies and institutes in 19 countries were working on vaccines, most gene-based instead of using traditional approaches, such as those that have been employed in influenza vaccines for more than 70 years. The labs predicted that a commercial vaccine could be available for emergency or compassionate use by early 2021—incredibly fast, given that vaccines to brand-new pathogens have taken a decade to be perfected and deployed.[25]

The global effort was unusually complicated by pandemic conditions. Some laboratories had closed due to the pandemic, and others were operating under pandemic restrictions. It was difficult for scientists to work together in person. The processes of manufacturing and vaccinating people were also unusually complicated for the same reason.

The mRNA Vaccine

Before the coronavirus emerged in 2020, Kizzmekia Corbett, a viral immunologist, was part of a team designing and testing vaccines for the National Institute of Allergy and Infectious Diseases (NIAID), a research agency of the US government. Corbett had worked on and tested vaccines for earlier coronaviruses. When the new deadly coronavirus emerged and the pandemic hit, Corbett and her team quickly started developing an mRNA vaccine for COVID-19.

It was an ambitious endeavor. Corbett was determined to develop not only a vaccine but also a strategy for vaccines in the

WHO director-general Tedros Adhanom Ghebreyesus (pictured at a 2019 conference) made a vaccine prediction that was widely considered to be overly optimistic. The reality turned out to be better than his prediction.

future. In December 2020 she spoke about the global effort to develop mRNA vaccines:

> Because coronavirus is always poised for human emergence, we need a vaccine that is fast . . . something that has the technology to be produced in vast quantities very quickly; reliable . . . a technology that has been tested in humans and upholds some level of manufacturability standards; universal . . . something that could at least provide a "plug-and-play strategy" if an outbreak should occur.[26]

The NIAID team isolated genetic material from the coronavirus and "plugged" it into the existing mRNA technology to create the COVID-19 vaccine, which was then produced by Moderna, a small US biotech company. The new vaccine was ready very quickly, but mRNA vaccines were still unproven. Similar vaccines for other diseases had been tested in humans but not in large-scale clinical trials. When the Moderna vaccine was ready, it was quickly administered to volunteers in clinical trials so it could be tested for safety and effectiveness.

In October 2020 journalist Elle Hardy volunteered to be one of the thirty thousand test subjects for the Moderna vaccine. The preparation for the testing was thorough. Hardy says, "Before I got the jab, I had to go through a lot of checks to make sure I was in good health for an experimental (at this stage) treatment. They went through my medical history, reviewed my medications, took my blood pressure and pulse, gave me a pregnancy test, and took eight vials of blood. They monitor its effects by blood samples throughout the trial."[27]

Hardy experienced a few predictable aftereffects, likely from the vaccine: soreness in her arm at the vaccination spot and mild flu-like symptoms. When the coronavirus vaccines were later rolled out to the public, 70 percent of those who received it experienced similar aftereffects. Although uncomfortable, these effects were far less troublesome than a real case of COVID-19.

Before the end of 2020, news from the clinical trials emerged: at least in the short term, the success rate of the new vaccine was higher than 90 percent in preventing COVID-19 infection, and even higher in preventing severe illness and death. Corbett and her team had succeeded.

A Multinational Vaccine Effort

Moderna's vaccine was not the only successful mRNA vaccine. Another resulted from a global partnership between Pfizer, an internationally known American drugmaker, and BioNTech, a small German biotech company founded by vaccine scientists Özlem Türeci and Ugur Sahin.

Over breakfast one morning in January 2020, Türeci talked with her spouse and partner, Sahin, about the coronavirus that had begun to spread in China. Turkish immigrants to Germany, Türeci and Sahin had been researching vaccine technology for two decades. On that morning in January 2020, they decided

COVAX and the Equitable Distribution of Vaccine

When vaccines became available at the end of 2020, the vaccine supply was dominated by wealthy countries that bought up many millions of doses from the manufacturers. Stopping the spread of the coronavirus and ending the suffering would require a worldwide vaccination effort. In an effort to make sure that everyone in the world has access to a vaccine, the WHO and several charitable groups formed a global initiative called COVAX.

Determined that the COVID-19 vaccines be equitably distributed around the world, COVAX worked with wealthy nations and some vaccine manufacturers to provide low-cost COVID-19 vaccines to developing countries. In the first months of 2021, COVAX shipped tens of millions of COVID-19 vaccines to sixty participant countries. The first recipient country was Ghana, on February 24, 2021, followed by other early recipients—Algeria, Malawi, Uganda, El Salvador, Nicaragua, Afghanistan, Iran, and Iraq, among others. The goal of COVAX was to distribute 2 billion doses of COVID-19 vaccine in 2021.

together to use their skills and knowledge to create a vaccine for the new coronavirus.

It was a risky business decision, but the couple saw an opportunity to save lives and stop a pandemic. When Türeci, the company's chief medical officer, was asked about their decision later, she said, "It pays off to make bold decisions and to trust that if you have an extraordinary team, you will be able to solve any problem and obstacle which comes your way."[28]

In March 2020 BioNTech partnered with Pfizer to develop, manufacture, and distribute an mRNA vaccine for COVID-19. Funding from Fosun Pharma, a Chinese company, made the partnership truly multinational. Preparation and testing were done quickly, and months later the results of clinical trials were announced: like the Moderna vaccine, the Pfizer-BioNTech vaccine had a success rate higher than 90 percent in preventing COVID-19 infection and even higher in preventing severe illness and death. The vaccine would be administered to millions of people in countries all over the world. It was one of the most successful of the cooperative, international responses to the coronavirus pandemic of 2020.

Speed and Safety

Because the creation of vaccines went at such a fast pace, skeptics around the world became concerned that safety would be neglected in the hurry to vaccinate people and stop the pandemic. Vaccine researchers and other experts noted that the effort was helped by the fact that Chinese scientists quickly shared the genetic sequence of the new coronavirus. When the information was released in January 2020, scientists worldwide immediately started to work on vaccines. In addition, research groups quickly obtained the funding they needed. Recognizing the urgency of the effort, governments around the globe funded the research in advance. And although vaccine developers fulfilled all the usual scientific requirements for vaccines, in order to finish as quickly as possible, they took some of the steps simultaneously.

Vaccine developers were able to quickly find volunteers for large-scale clinical trials because the public wanted to help with the effort. When people were injected with vaccines, they were closely monitored, both in clinical trials and after the vaccines had been approved for emergency use. And governments worldwide required the vaccine makers to prove their products safe and effective before authorizing them for emergency use. Vaccines were the only way to stop the pandemic, and infectious disease experts repeatedly commented that the health risks of COVID-19 far outweighed the health risks of the vaccines.

Vaccinating the Whole World

Countries all over the world had invested billions to create, test, and manufacture vaccines in record time. The next step was to vaccinate the global population, to inject the precious vaccines into the arms of people. As vaccines were authorized for use in countries around the world, manufacturers hurried to meet the growing demand. Quickly vaccinating billions of people and stopping the spread of COVID-19 represented an enormous challenge.

Vaccine rollout, which began in December 2020, had a bumpy start. The supply of vaccine doses could not meet the demand, and when supply became available, many governments scrambled to prepare. They did not have the logistical resources—funding, storage space, or staff—to receive and deliver vaccines to the population under pandemic conditions. Health care workers and facilities were already overwhelmed. For countries with poor roads and unreliable power service, the challenges were even greater. By the end of 2020, about 10 million vaccinations had been given worldwide, only a tiny fraction of the numbers needed for a global population of 7.8 billion. It was only the beginning.

A Southern California man receives the one-shot Johnson & Johnson COVID-19 vaccine in March 2021. Vaccine rollout, which began in December 2020, had a bumpy start—and some countries fared much better than others.

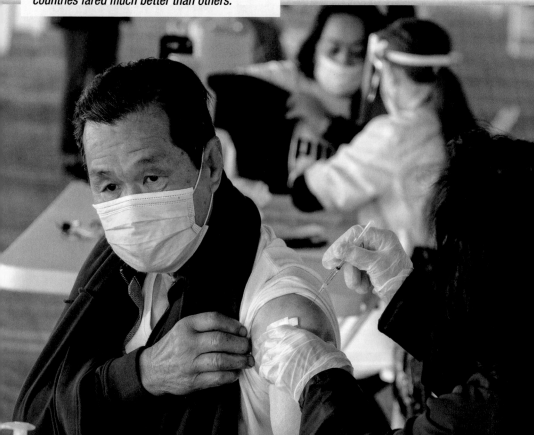

Governments began vaccinating groups of people in waves, starting with categories of people at the front of the vaccination line: those at high risk for illness and death from COVID-19 and those at high risk of exposure and transmission—health care workers and others who kept society running. Most countries gave their first vaccines to health care workers and elderly people. In the first months of 2021, hundreds of millions of people were vaccinated. However, vaccines were not equitably shared around the world. Rich countries like the United Kingdom and the United States had access to more than their share of vaccines because, according to BBC News, "they could afford to invest a lot of money into vaccine development and put themselves at the front of the queue."[29]

Short supply was not the only problem. Fear and suspicion made some people reluctant to receive vaccinations that had been developed so quickly. Where people were hesitant and afraid, some world leaders stepped up and set the example to encourage others. In early March 2021 the Dalai Lama, the spiritual leader of Tibet, had his vaccination recorded on video and then turned to the camera to gently deliver a message to the world: "More people should have the courage to take this injection."[30]

Joshua Barocas, an infectious disease specialist in Boston, was on the front lines during the early days of the pandemic and stayed away from his family to keep them safe from the coronavirus. After a long, difficult year fighting COVID-19 in 2020, Barocas wept when he received his vaccination. He says:

I cried because I was overwhelmed by grief, but I also cried because of the enormity of the moment. In under a year, scientists developed not just one, but multiple vaccines against a virus that was previously unknown. They used new technology and collaborated across the globe with a single unified vision—defeat the virus. And with the help of brave people who volunteered for clinical trials, they did it.[31]

Samantha Hallgren, a registered nurse at a nursing home for veterans in the Canadian capital of Ottawa, cared for residents with COVID-19 throughout 2020. Hallgren cared for patients as they died without the comfort of their families. It was a difficult year. When it was her turn to be vaccinated, Hallgren was relieved and overwhelmed. "When I got the call to go get the vaccine, I sobbed and sobbed,"[32] she says.

Herd Immunity

At the end of 2020, scientists estimated that about 10 percent of the world's population had already developed some natural immunity to the coronavirus. These were people who had been sick and whose immune systems had defeated the COVID-19 infection. But 10 percent is not nearly enough to achieve herd immunity. Herd immunity occurs when a high percentage of the population, usually more than 70 percent, is immune to a disease. When the population reaches herd immunity, the spread of disease is greatly reduced. The human population has achieved herd immunity worldwide, historically, with such diseases as smallpox, measles, and polio. But the only way to achieve this level of immunity is through global vaccination campaigns.

As large numbers of people were vaccinated in late 2020 and continuing into 2021, the number of infections began to decline in regions where mass vaccinations were occurring. Elsewhere, though, the coronavirus continued to spread. Herd immunity would take time, and difficulties remained. Vaccinating 70 percent of the world's population was an enormous challenge that would involve addressing health care disparities worldwide. The pandemic had not ended, and many challenges lay ahead, but the vaccines offered hope in 2021.

SOURCE NOTES

Introduction: The Coronavirus Emerged

1. Quoted in Amy Qin et al., "Voices from China's Covid-19 Crisis: 'If I Survive This, What Will I Do?,'" *New York Times*, December 30, 2020. www.nytimes.com.
2. Quoted in Donald G. McNeil Jr., "Fauci on What Working for Trump Was Really Like," *New York Times*, January 24, 2021. www.nytimes.com.

Chapter One: The Coronavirus Circled the Globe

3. Quoted in Christopher Brito, "Spring Breakers Say Coronavirus Pandemic Won't Stop Them from Partying," CBS News, March 18, 2020. www.cbsnews.com.
4. Quoted in Richard Read, "A Mount Vernon Choir Went Ahead with Rehearsal. Now Dozens Have Coronavirus and 2 Are Dead," *Seattle (WA) Times*, March 29, 2020. www.seattletimes.com.
5. Joris Lammers et al., "Correcting Misperceptions of Exponential Coronavirus Growth," *Proceedings of the National Academy of Sciences of the United States of America*, July 14, 2020. www.pnas.org.
6. Quoted in World Health Organization, "WHO Director-General's Statement on the Advice of the IHR Emergency Committee on Novel Coronavirus," January 23, 2020. www.who.int.
7. Quoted in World Health Organization, "Statement on the Second Meeting of the International Health Regulations (2005) Emergency Committee Regarding the Outbreak of Novel Coronavirus (2019-nCoV)," January 30, 2020. www.who.int.
8. Quoted in Lori Rozsa et al., "The Battle over Masks in a Pandemic: An All-American Story," *Washington Post*, June 19, 2020. www.washingtonpost.com.

9. Quoted in Matt Kawahara, "Why Do Some People Refuse to Wear Masks? Defiance, Misguided Thinking," *San Francisco (CA) Chronicle*, May 31, 2020. www.sfchronicle.com.
10. Quoted in Douglas Starr, "How Italy's 'Father of the Swabs' Fought the Coronavirus," *Science*, August 27, 2020. www.sciencemag.org.

Chapter Two: A Year of Pandemic Suffering

11. Quoted in Johns Hopkins Medicine, "US Coronavirus and COVID-19 Recovery: Theirrien's Story," 2021. www.hopkinsmedicine.org.
12. Ariana Eunjung Cha, "A Mysterious Blood-Clotting Complication Is Killing Coronavirus Patients," *Washington Post*, April 22, 2020. www.washingtonpost.com.
13. Cha, "A Mysterious Blood-Clotting Complication Is Killing Coronavirus Patients."
14. Quoted in Reed Abelson, "Covid Overload: U.S. Hospitals Are Running Out of Beds for Patients," *New York Times*, November 27, 2020. www.nytimes.com.
15. Quoted in Andrew Harding, "Coronavirus in South Africa: Inside Port Elizabeth's 'Hospitals of Horrors,'" BBC News, July 15, 2020. www.bbc.com.
16. Lydia Smith, "Woman's Entire Family Dies After She Hides Positive COVID Test," *Newsweek*, February 4, 2021. www.newsweek.com.
17. Daniel Burke, "Coronavirus Preys on What Terrifies Us: Dying Alone," CNN, March 29, 2020. www.cnn.com.

Chapter Three: Pandemic Shock to the Global Economy

18. Jerome Taylor, "Viral Hysteria: Hong Kong Coronavirus Panic Sparks Run on Toilet Paper," Hong Kong Free Press, February 6, 2020. https://hongkongfp.com.
19. Quoted in Zeba Siddiqui and Sunil Kataria, "'Some of Us Will Die': India's Homeless Stranded by Coronavirus Lockdown," Reuters, April 1, 2020. www.reuters.com.
20. Quoted in Yolande Knell, "Egypt Desperate to Revive Coronavirus-Hit Tourism Industry," BBC News, July 15, 2020. www.bbc.com.

21. Quoted in Knell, "Egypt Desperate to Revive Coronavirus-Hit Tourism Industry."
22. Quoted in Benjamin Katz et al., "From Pilot to Truck Driver—Airline Careers Grounded by Pandemic," *Wall Street Journal*, December 7, 2020. www.wsj.com.
23. Quoted in Mary Abbajay, "3 Inspiring Small Business Stories on How to Survive During Covid-19," *Forbes*, May 21, 2020. www.forbes.com.

Chapter Four: Vaccines to the Rescue

24. Quoted in World Health Organization, "WHO Director-General's Remarks at the Media Briefing on 2019-nCoV on 11 February 2020," February 11, 2020. www.who.int.
25. Charles Schmidt, "Genetic Engineering Could Make a COVID-19 Vaccine in Months Rather than Years," *Scientific American*, June 1, 2020. www.scientificamerican.com.
26. Quoted in Carla Garnett, "Fast, Reliable, Universal: Corbett Recounts Quest for Covid Vaccine," *NIH Record*, December 11, 2020. https://nihrecord.nih.gov.
27. Elle Hardy, "I Volunteered to Test the Moderna Coronavirus Vaccine," Business Insider, January 8, 2021. www.businessinsider.com.
28. Quoted in Frank Jordans, "Scientist Behind Coronavirus Shot Says Next Target Is Cancer," Associated Press, March 20, 2021. https://apnews.com.
29. Stephanie Hegarty, "Covid Vaccine Tracker: How's My Country and the Rest of the World Doing?," BBC News, February 12, 2021. www.bbc.com.
30. Quoted in Office of His Holiness the Dalai Lama, "His Holiness the Dalai Lama Receives COVID-19 Vaccine," March 6, 2021. www.dalailama.com.
31. Joshua Barocas, "Pulled by Hope and Grief: What It Felt like to Get the Vaccine," WBUR, December 17, 2020. www.wbur.org.
32. Quoted in Catherine Porter, "In Canada, First Vaccines Leave Health Workers in Tears of Relief," *New York Times*, December 14, 2020. www.nytimes.com.

FOR FURTHER RESEARCH

Books

Richard Horton, *The COVID-19 Catastrophe: What's Gone Wrong and How to Stop It Happening Again*. Cambridge, UK: Polity, 2020.

Debora MacKenzie, *COVID-19: The Pandemic That Never Should Have Happened and How to Stop the Next One*. New York: Hachette, 2020.

Michael Mosley, *COVID-19: Everything You Need to Know About the Corona Virus and the Race for the Vaccine*. New York: Atria, 2020.

Delthia Ricks, *100 Questions & Answers About Coronaviruses*. Burlington, MA: Jones & Bartlett Learning, 2021.

Bradley Steffens, *Health, Illness, and Death in the Time of COVID-19*. San Diego, CA: ReferencePoint, 2021.

Internet Sources

Gina Kolata, "Coronavirus Is Very Different from the Spanish Flu of 1918. Here's How," *New York Times*, March 16, 2020. www.nytimes.com.

Amy McKeever, "Here's What Coronavirus Does to the Body," *National Geographic*, February 18, 2020. www.nationalgeographic.com.

Siobhan Roberts, "Flattening the Coronavirus Curve: One Chart Explains Why Slowing the Spread of the Infection Is Nearly as Important as Stopping It," *New York Times*, March 27, 2020. www.nytimes.com.

Derrick Bryson Taylor, "A Timeline of the Coronavirus Pandemic," *New York Times*, March 17, 2021. www.nytimes.com.

Visual and Data Journalism Team, "Covid Map: Coronavirus Cases, Deaths, Vaccinations by Country," BBC News, 2021. www.bbc.com.

Nadav Ziv and Sam Wineburg, "How to Spot Coronavirus Misinformation," *Time*, March 16, 2020. https://time.com.

Websites
Centers for Disease Control and Prevention (CDC)
www.cdc.gov/coronavirus/2019-ncov

The CDC is the nation's premier public health protection agency. The agency's website devotes significant space to coronavirus and COVID-19 facts and statistics. The site also has extensive information on who is at risk, protective measures, contact tracing, community response, schools and youth, and more.

Johns Hopkins Coronavirus Resource Center (CRC)
https://coronavirus.jhu.edu

The CRC, created and run by Johns Hopkins University & Medicine, is a continuously updated source of COVID-19 data and expert guidance. The center gathers and analyzes statistics and other information related to COVID-19 cases, testing, contact tracing, and vaccine research. The site also provides links to numerous articles from a variety of sources.

National Institute of Allergy and Infectious Diseases (NIAID)
www.niaid.nih.gov

The NIAID is one of the twenty-seven institutes and centers that make up the National Institutes of Health. Its website includes information about coronaviruses, the public health and government response to COVID-19, and treatment guidelines. It also provides details on volunteering for prevention clinical studies.

National Institutes of Health (NIH)

www.nih.gov/coronavirus

Part of the US Department of Health and Human Services, the NIH is the largest biomedical research agency in the world. Its website provides information on the development of COVID-19 vaccines, testing, and treatments, as well as links to other related topics.

US Food and Drug Administration (FDA)

www.fda.gov

The FDA regulates drugs, medical devices, and other products and oversees food safety. Its website provides pandemic-related statistics and information on protective equipment, treatments, and testing. It includes an extensive section of frequently asked questions about a variety of COVID-19 topics.

World Health Organization (WHO)

www.who.int/emergencies/diseases/novel-coronavirus-2019

Working within the framework of the United Nations, the WHO directs and coordinates global health issues. Its website features rolling coronavirus updates, situation reports, travel advice, facts about preventive measures such as masks, information on how the virus spreads, and more.

INDEX

Note: Boldface page numbers indicate illustrations.

Adel, Shahenda, 38
air travel, 11–12
assisted living facilities, 29
AstraZeneca and Oxford University
vaccine, 44
asymptomatic transmission, 8, 14
attenuated-virus vaccines, 44

Barocas, Joshua, 53
basketball (professional), 15
bats, 19
BBC News, 53
BioNTech, 49–50
Bollywood, 37
Bond, Shannon, 39
Burke, Daniel, 29
business and industry
crash of financial markets, 33–34
film industry, 37
global contraction of, 32–33, **33**, 37
government aid, 42
New York City, **33**
oil, 39–40
online shopping, 42
remote work, 36
restaurant and food service, 40–41, **41**
retail, 41–42
supply and demand problems, 34–35, **35**
tourism and travel industries, 37–39
unemployment, 36–37
videoconferencing by, 39

Cha, Ariana Eunjung, 24, 25
Clark, Theirrien, 22–23
clotting syndrome, 24–25
Comstock, Carolynn, 14
contact tracing, 18–19
Corbett, Kizzmekia, 47–49
Cordero, Nick, 25
coronaviruses, **7**
COVAX, 50
COVID-19 pandemic
"long-haul" health effects, 31
named, 8
timeline, **4–5**
Crisanti, Andrea, 20
cytokine storms, 23, 28

Dalai Lama, 53
deaths
among health care workers and
support staff, 25–26
dying without family, 29, 54
global
by January 2020, 9
by February 2020, 11
December 31, 2020, 16, 21
locations, 31
per infections, 23
US
December 31, 2020, 16
March 2020, 12
"super-spreader" events, 13–14
depression, 29–31, **30**

e-commerce, 42
economy, global. *See* business
and industry

education, 30
energy industry, 39–40

fast-food restaurants, 41
Fauci, Anthony, 9
film industry, 37
financial markets, global crash of,
   33–34
food service industry, 40–41, **41**
Fosun Pharma, 50
Fuentes, Verónica García, 27–28

Ghebreyesus, Tedros Adhanom, 16,
   45, **47**
global economy. *See* business and
   industry
Guardian (British newspaper), 25

Hallgren, Samantha, 54
Hardy, Elle, 48
Harper, Greg, 38–39
health care systems
   fear of being overwhelmed, 16
   infections and deaths among health
     care workers and support staff,
     25–26
   overwhelmed hospitals described,
     25, 26–27
   protective equipment, **27**
herd immunity, 54
Hong Kong Free Press (website), 35
Howard, Jeremy, 18
Hussain, Zakir, 36

immune system
   cytokine storms, 23, 28
   defenses, 43–44, **45**
   new pathogens and, 7
incubation period, 14
industry. *See* business and industry
infections
   among health care workers and
     support staff, 25–26
   global
     by January 2020, 9
     by February 2020, 11
     December 31, 2020, 16, 21

in lungs, 23–24, **24**
range of severity of, 23
US by December 31, 2020, 16
International Energy Agency, 40
International Monetary Fund, 33
Israel, 49

James, LeBron, 15
Johns Hopkins Coronavirus Resource
   Center, 16, 21
Johnson & Johnson and Jansen
   vaccine, 44, **52**
*Journal of the American Medical
   Association*, 29–30

Kaiser Health News, 25
Kaminski, Steve, 29

"long-haul" COVID-19, 31
Los Angeles Times (newspaper), 37

masks, **17**, 18
mental health, 29–31, **30**
messenger RNA (mRNA) vaccines, 44,
   47–50
Moderna, 48

Nasr, Ashraf, 38
National Academy of Sciences, 14
National Basketball Association (NBA),
   15
National Restaurant Association, 40
"NBA bubble," 15
Newsweek (magazine), 28
nursing homes, 29

oil industry, 39–40
Olympics, 38
online shopping, 42
Osterholm, Michael, 25
Oxford University, 44

Pabatao, Alfredo, 25, 26
Pabatao, Susana, 25–26
pangolins, 19
Parsell, Max, 18
pathogens and immune system, 7

Pfizer, 49, 50
pollution, decrease in, 40
public health prevention strategies, **17**, 17–19

quarantine, 18–19, 20–21

respiratory illness
  causes of, 6–7
  COVID-19 in lungs, 23–24, **24**
restaurant and food service industry, 40–41, **41**
retail businesses, 41–42

Sahin, Ugur, 49–50
SARS-CoV-2 (severe acute respiratory syndrome coronavirus 2)
  genetic sequence of, 51
  source of, 8, 19
Schmidt, Charles, 46
science, 9
Scientific American (magazine), 46
severe acute respiratory syndrome (SARS), 7, 8
Sinovac vaccine, 44
Smith, Lydia, 28
social distancing, **17**, 17–18
Sodidi, Khaya, 27
Sputnik V vaccine, 44
Stern, Bettina, 40–41
"super-spreader" events, 13–14
supply and demand of products, 34–35, **35**

testing, 18
toilet paper shortages, 33, **35**
tourism and travel industries, 37–39
transmission
  asymptomatic, 8, 14
  methods of, 8, 11–13
  public health strategies to slow, **17**, 17–19
  route of, 10–11, **12**
  speed of, 9, 10, 14–15
  "super-spreader" events, 13–14

surges and, 21
Türeci, Özlem, 49–50

United States
  deaths
    March 2020, 12
    December 31, 2020, 16
    "super-spreader" events, 13–14
  infections by December 31, 2020, 16

vaccinations, **52**
  described, 44
  in Israel, 49
  number of, by end of 2020, 52
  percentage of, by end of 2020, 54
  procedures used, 53
  publicizing, 53
vaccines
  aftereffects, 48
  approaches used, 44, 47–50
  described, 44
  development time, 45–47, 51
  equitable distribution of, 50, 53
  funding, 51
  rollout of, 52, **52**
  skeptics, 51
  testing safety of, 48, 51
videoconferences, 39
viral-vector vaccines, 44
Vo, Italy, 19–21

Washington Post (newspaper), 24, 25
World Health Organization (WHO)
  equitable distribution of vaccines, 50
  official coronavirus name, 8
  spread outside of China, 15–16
Wuhan, China, 6, 8

youth, depression among, 29–31, **30**
Yuan, Eric, 39

Zhang Yongzhen, 7, 8
Zoom, 39

PICTURE CREDITS